UNRAVELLING THE CLASSICAL ELEMENTS

By
Dominic Bayor

Unravelling The Classical Elements

Copyright © 2025 Dominic Bayor

All rights reserved. This book or any portion thereof may not be reproduced or used in any manner whatsoever without the express written permission of the publisher except for the use of brief quotations in a book review.

Published by: London Book Publisher

TABLE OF CONTENTS

ACKNOWLEDGEMENTS iv

INTRODUCTION v

CHAPTER 1 The Composition Of Human Kind 1

CHAPTER 2 The Spirit, The Soul, And The Body 9

CHAPTER 3 The Nature Of Angels 14

CHAPTER 4 The Element Of The Earth 18

CHAPTER 5 The Element Of The Air 29

CHAPTER 6 The Element Of Fire 33

CHAPTER 7 The Element Of Water 44

CHAPTER 8 Purification Of Our Works 46

CHAPTER 9 The Elements And Their Corresponding Household Characteristics 48

CHAPTE 10 Diverse Ministerial Paths Aligned With Elemental Traits. 51

CHAPTER 11 Living Above The Elements 58

CHAPTER 12 The Legacy Of Remarkable Men And Women Of God 65

CHAPTER 13 The Call To Greater Works 69

ACKNOWLEDGEMENTS

I would like to dedicate this book, **Unravelling the Classical Elements,** to my father, Mr. Edward Bayor, whose unwavering love, guidance, and support have been the bedrock of my journey. From the earliest moments of my life, your presence has been a constant source of strength and inspiration. Your belief in me, even during times when I doubted myself, has shaped the person I am today.

You have always been there, offering wisdom when needed, a listening ear when I sought advice, and a steady hand when the path seemed uncertain. Your dedication to nurturing my dreams and your patience in helping me grow have been instrumental in my pursuit of knowledge and my passion for discovery. This book is as much yours as it is mine, for it is your love and sacrifice that made it possible.

Thank you, Dad, for being my greatest teacher and my greatest supporter. I will forever be grateful for the foundation you have given me, and I dedicate every word within these pages to you.

INTRODUCTION

In the opening verses of Genesis 1:1-2, we are introduced to the foundational elements of the universe: ***"In the beginning, God created the heaven and the earth. And the earth was without form and void; darkness was upon the face of the deep. And the Spirit of God moved upon the face of the waters."*** Here, within the very fabric of creation, we discover the classical elements: fire, earth, air, and water—each a manifestation of divine wisdom and the inherent order of the universe. The Hebrew word for "heaven" is "shamayim," and it simply means "fire" or "light," suggesting that, from the very outset, the "Kosmos" (world) itself can be understood as an intricate tapestry woven from these elements. Fire embodies passion, drive, and transformation; air stands for intellect, communication, and breath; earth signifies stability, growth, and nourishment; water reflects emotion, intuition, and renewal. These elements are not merely passive forces but interconnected, dynamic expressions of the order of creation.

Despite their profound significance, many Christians hesitate to explore the classical elements, often dismissing them as secular or incompatible with their faith. This reluctance is intriguing, especially considering that these elements are fundamental to secular education and our understanding of the natural world. How can we, as people of faith, neglect to explore the very building blocks of creation as part of our pursuit of divine knowledge? There is no inherent conflict between studying the elements and deepening our spiritual awareness. Although disciplines like medicine, business, and science are often regarded as secular, they can seamlessly integrate with faith, as they coexist harmoniously with belief in a higher power.

Embracing the study of elements within the context of our Christian faith can deepen our understanding of God's wisdom and reveal the interconnectedness of all truth. When approached with reverence and insight, they can illuminate our path, helping us align more fully with God's will while offering profound revelations about our personal growth, relationships, and purpose. This book invites you on a transformative journey that reveals the sacredness of the elements and their profound connection to the very fabric of our existence. As you explore these pages, you will discover how the elements guide us toward a life of balance, clarity, and divine alignment.

CHAPTER 1
The Composition Of Human Kind

Every human being is composed of four elements: fire, earth, air, and water. These elemental forms correspond to soul, body, spirit, and blood. Despite these commonalities in our makeup, one element distinguishes each person, serving as their unique identity. Understanding this fundamental distinction is crucial for preventing identity crises, appreciating our unique personalities, and making informed decisions. To fully understand our identity in relation to our birth, we must view time from God's perspective, rather than relying solely on the Gregorian or Julian calendar. The Hebrew calendar, which reflects divine timing, designates Nissan as the first month of the year, corresponding to March-April in the Gregorian calendar. While this perspective may seem unconventional to many believers, it is clearly outlined in Scripture.

Exodus 12:2(KJV) states, *"This month shall be unto you the beginning of months: it shall be the first month of the year to you."* Thus, Nissan (March-April) marks the beginning of the year, while Adar (February-March) concludes it as the twelfth month. The sequence of months is as follows: Nissan, Iyar, Sivan, Tammuz, Av, Elul, Tishrei, Cheshvan, Kislev, Tevet, Shevat, and Adar. By recognizing our birth month within the framework of the Hebrew calendar, we align our understanding of identity with God's appointed timing and purposes for our lives. This alignment invites us to view our lives through the lens of divine order, enriching our sense of purpose and connection to His eternal plan.

Unravelling The Classical Elements

Below are the tabulated zodiac signs, their respective houses, and their elemental associations:

Zodiac Sign	Months	House	Element
Aries	March 21st - April 20th	House 1	Fire
Taurus	April 21st - May 20th	House 2	Earth
Gemini	May 21st - June 20th	House 3	Air
Cancer	June 21st - July 22nd	House 4	Water
Leo	July 23rd - August 22nd	House 5	Fire
Virgo	August 23rd - September 22nd	House 6	Earth
Libra	September 23rd - October 22nd	House 7	Air
Scorpio	October 23rd - November 21st	House 8	Water
Sagittarius	November 22nd - December 21st	House 9	Fire
Capricorn	December 22nd - January 19th	House 10	Earth
Aquarius	January 20th - February 18th	House 11	Air
Pisces	February 19th - March 20th	House 12	Water

Understanding our elemental identities is both a philosophical journey and a practical framework. It invites us to explore the core forces that shape who we are—our nature, instincts, and inner balance.

By recognizing the unique combination of influences that shape us, we gain valuable insights into our personalities, abilities, and potential for growth. This self-awareness serves as the foundation for personal growth, enabling us to harness our strengths, address areas for improvement, and align our professional lives with our passions and talents.

It also empowers us to face challenges with resilience, make informed decisions, and seize opportunities confidently, fostering greater fulfillment and a stronger sense of purpose and direction. Embarking on the journey of understanding our elemental identities is not just an exercise but a transformative experience. It is a journey that unlocks our potential, enabling us to live authentically, grow profoundly, and lead meaningful lives.

CHARACTERISTICS OF EACH OF THE ZODIAC SIGNS

Aries (March 21st - April 20th):

Aries, symbolized by the Ram, is a dynamic fire sign renowned for its assertiveness, boldness, and leadership capabilities. Individuals born under this sign have a pioneering spirit, are constantly driven by ambition, and have an ardent desire for new challenges. Aries excels in environments that demand quick thinking, decisiveness, and action. Their natural ability to take risks and lead others makes them exceptional in competitive fields, where their enthusiasm and courage inspire others to follow suit.

Taurus (April 21st - May 20th):

Taurus, represented by the Bull, is an earth sign known for its unwavering stability, patience, and practicality. Taureans are dependable individuals who thrive in cultivating lasting foundations in both personal and professional spheres. Their strong work ethic and attention to detail make them adept at creating tangible results, especially in roles that require consistency and perseverance. As lovers of comfort and beauty, they excel in environments that allow them to build security and enhance the quality of life for themselves and others.

Gemini (May 21st - June 20th):

Gemini, symbolized by the Twins, is an air sign celebrated for its adaptability, intellect, and communication skills. Geminis' adaptability and ability to easily navigate a wide range of ideas, environments, and people are fascinating aspects of their personality. Their curiosity and versatility make them skilled communicators, networkers, and problem solvers. Their dynamic nature thrives on variety and mental stimulation, which drives them to excel in communication, teaching, and creative exploration.

Cancer (June 21st - July 22nd):

The Crab is Cancer, a water sign marked by emotional depth, intuition, and a nurturing disposition. Cancerians' nurturing nature, empathy, and ability to easily attune to the emotional undercurrents of their environment are comforting aspects of their personality. Their natural ability to offer support and create a sense of security makes them ideal in caregiving or counselling roles. They have a deep connection to home and family, strengthening their ability to foster meaningful bonds and offer compassionate guidance. Their creativity and intuitive wisdom further enhance their ability to inspire and heal.

Leo (July 23rd - August 22nd):

Leo, symbolized by the Lion, is a fire sign known for its commanding presence, charisma, and innate leadership. The leadership qualities of Leos, as well as their confidence and vitality, often draw others to them with natural enthusiasm and passion. They excel in roles that allow them to lead, inspire, and express themselves creatively. With a deep sense of self-worth and pride, Leos thrive in environments where they can take center stage, make a lasting impact, and encourage others to reach their highest potential. Their vibrant personalities and passion for life make them born entertainers and motivators.

Virgo (August 23rd - September 22nd):

Virgo, represented by the Virgin, is an earth sign known for its precision, analytical mind, and deep commitment to service. Virgos are meticulous and discerning individuals who excel in organizing and refining systems to achieve efficiency and quality. Their keen attention to detail enables them to approach tasks precisely, ensuring that even minor aspects are not overlooked. Virgos thrive in roles that require methodical planning, problem-solving and a commitment to improvement, particularly in research, healthcare, and management positions.

Libra (September 23rd - October 22nd):

Libra, symbolized by the Scales, is an air sign associated with diplomacy, harmony, and a deep sense of justice. Librans are naturally charming and sociable individuals who seek balance and peace in their relationships and surroundings. Their ability to understand different perspectives makes them effective mediators and negotiators, skilled at fostering cooperation and resolving conflicts. Libras are drawn to roles that involve building connections, promoting fairness, and enhancing communal well-being, excelling in environments where collaboration and mutual understanding are key.

Scorpio (October 23rd - November 21st):

Scorpio, symbolized by the Scorpion, is a water sign renowned for its intensity, passion, and resilience. Scorpios have an unyielding inner strength and the ability to confront life's complexities with remarkable depth and insight. They are naturally inclined to explore hidden truths and transform challenges into opportunities for growth. Scorpios thrive in roles that demand emotional intelligence, strategic thinking, and the ability to navigate complex emotional landscapes. Their loyalty, determination, and transformative energy make them excellent leaders and problem-solvers in high-stakes environments.

Sagittarius (November 22nd - December 21st):

The Archer represents Sagittarius as a fire sign characterized by its adventurous spirit, optimism, and philosophical nature. Sagittarians are freedom-loving individuals who seek exploration in the physical world and the realms of ideas. They have a broad vision and a deep curiosity that propels them toward continuous learning and personal growth. Their infectious enthusiasm and zest for life inspire others to embrace change and diligently pursue their dreams. Sagittarians excel in roles that involve travel, teaching, or entrepreneurship, where their love for discovery can be fully realized.

Capricorn (December 22nd - January 19th):

Capricorn, symbolized by the Goat, is an earth sign known for its discipline, ambition, and resilience. Capricorns are pragmatic individuals who set long-term goals and work tirelessly to achieve them. Their methodical approach to life and work ensures they can navigate obstacles steadily. Capricorns shine in roles that demand leadership, strategic thinking, and commitment to success. Their ability to manage resources effectively and their strong sense of responsibility make them well-suited for positions of authority where their dedication to excellence is appreciated.

Aquarius (January 20th - February 18th):

Aquarius, symbolized by the Water Bearer, is an air sign renowned for its originality, independence, and progressive ideals. Aquarians are forward-thinking individuals who are often ahead of their time, driven by a desire to challenge norms and create innovative solutions. They have a sharp intellect and an unwavering commitment to social justice, often advocating for change and equality. Aquarians excel in roles that involve technology, activism, or visionary work, where their creativity and commitment to societal progress can make a tangible impact on the world.

Pisces (February 19th - March 20th):

Pisces, represented by the Fish, is a water sign known for its compassion, creativity, and intuitive abilities. Pisceans are deeply empathetic and often attuned to the emotions and energies of others. Their strong intuition allows them to navigate complex emotional landscapes, making them exceptional in roles that require sensitivity and understanding. They have a profound connection to art, spirituality, and healing, and their creative expression flows naturally from their deep well of imagination. Pisceans excel in arts, counseling, and spiritual guidance, offering comfort and insight to those in need. Their wisdom, often beyond their years, enables them to support others meaningfully.

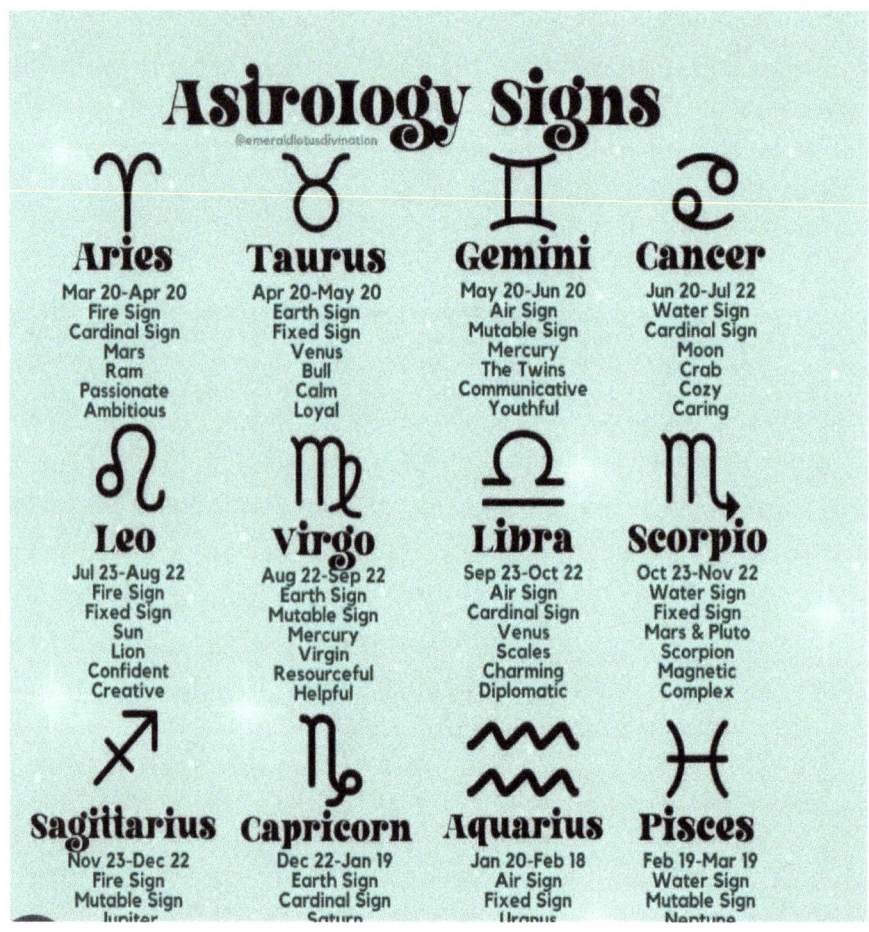

CHAPTER 2
The Spirit, The Soul, And The Body

The Human Spirit

The term "spirit" is derived from the Hebrew word *Ruach*, which means the breath or wind of God. This term signifies the vital essence of life, the animating force that sustains all existence. Intriguingly, this divine breath is associated with the element of air, symbolizing its intangible yet essential nature. The breath within us governs the rhythm of our lives, signifying vitality, and the animation of our being. Consider what the Word of God reveals: *"Then the Lord God formed a man from the dust of the ground and breathed into his nostrils the breath of life, and the man became a living being."* (Genesis 2:7). This verse poignantly illustrates how the divine breath that God breathed into Adam imparted to him the very gift of life. The human spirit emanates directly from God, the Father of all spirits. Hebrews 12:9 (KJV) affirms this truth: *"Furthermore we have had fathers of our flesh which corrected us, and we gave them reverence: shall we not much rather be in subjection unto the Father of spirits, and live?"*

This verse highlights our spiritual lineage and emphasizes our deep connection with God, our Creator and Sustainer. As the ultimate source of all life, God is our spiritual Father, uniting us as part of a greater spiritual whole. Just as the body has its faculties, the spirit possesses senses that enable it to perceive and engage with the spiritual realm. These faculties must be nurtured and developed to fully experience the spiritual dimensions of human existence.

Spiritual practices such as prayer, meditation, and fasting are vital disciplines through which we activate and fortify our spirit, much like physical exercise strengthens the body. These practices increase our awareness and receptivity to messages, guidance, and inspiration from God. Recognizing Him as the Father of our spirits deepens our understanding of our spiritual essence and origin, affirming our bond with Him and reinforcing our identity as His children. By embracing this understanding, we gain clarity about our spiritual identity and purpose, drawing strength from our connection with God. This insight inspires us to face life's challenges with renewed energy and resolve, living in alignment with His will and contributing meaningfully to His plan for our lives.

The Human Soul

The soul's origin remains a mystery, even though holy scriptures offer clear insights into the origins of the human spirit and body. Ecclesiastes 12:7 sheds light on this topic*: "**Then shall the dust return to the earth as it was: and the spirit shall return unto God who gave it**.*" This verse highlights the return of the physical body to the earth and the spirit to its divine source in God, but it does not explicitly address the source of the human soul. The soul unites these essential components, acting as a bridge between the spirit and the body. Rooted in the Hebrew term "nephesh," which means "a spark of light," the soul is linked to the element of fire—a dynamic and transformative force. It encompasses the core of human consciousness and identity, including the faculties of will, intellect, and emotion. Our soul is not merely a part of our being but a powerful force that shapes our thoughts, desires, and actions. It influences how we perceive the world, make decisions, and interact with others. As the source of our personality and the driving force behind our impulses and aspirations, the soul holds the potential for growth, evolution, and self-realization—much like fire's ability to transform.

The manifestation of our souls on earth is intentional, with each soul entrusted with a distinct assignment to carry out during its time here. This mission is not random, but a predetermined calling agreed upon before the soul's arrival. This understanding reminds us that our existence is meaningful and divinely guided, offering assurance and fostering confidence in our actions.

Our souls are dedicated to fulfilling the roles entrusted to us by God. This may involve personal transformation, selfless service to others, or significant contributions to the greater spiritual tapestry of existence. Each person bears the responsibility of discovering and aligning with their unique purpose, striving to live a life filled with meaning and impact. Embracing this journey with intention empowers us to shape our destiny and contribute to the transformation of the world around us.

In the Akan tradition, the term *"kra"* refers to the soul and signifies the divine permission to embark on one's sacred life mission. This concept underscores the deliberate and participatory nature of the soul's evolution on earth, suggesting that it plays an active role in its growth. As stewards of our souls, we are called to honor and fulfill the divine purpose for which we were created, ensuring that our lives reflect the sacred path we are destined to follow.

The Human Body

The human body's elemental composition is deeply rooted in the earth, with the earth serving as its foundational element while also incorporating fire, air, and water. According to the biblical narrative, the human form was shaped from clay, epitomizing its intrinsic connection to the natural world. Various body parts reflect this elemental composition: the eyes are made of water, the teeth and testicles are made from stone, and the rest of the body is formed from clay.

1 Corinthians 6:19 underscores the sacred nature of the human body: "What? know ye not that your body is the temple of the Holy Ghost, which is in you, which ye have of God, and ye are not your own?" This verse highlights the body's divinely ordained purpose and sanctity, affirming it as a vessel for God's presence. Likewise, in Matthew 26:61, Jesus speaks of His own body as the temple of God, stating, "And said, I can destroy the temple of God, and to build it in three days." This further reinforces the idea of the body as a sacred vessel for the divine.

The concept of humanity as a temple originates in the Garden of Eden, which was more than a physical space—it was a sacred temple with three distinct courts, symbolizing the convergence of spiritual and earthly realms. Humanity reflects this sacred design, as the outer court, the Holy Place, and the Most Holy Place of the Edenic temple correspond to the human body, soul, and spirit. The man was fashioned from this sacred structure, designed to be a vessel for God's presence.

Contrary to prevalent belief, Adam was not merely a gardener or farmer within Eden. He was entrusted with a priestly role, stewarding God's divine order and managing the sacred space where the physical and spiritual intertwined. This exemplifies humanity's original calling to honour and reflect God's design in all dimensions of life.

While humanity shares a common origin with the earth, its rich diversity in skin tones and physical characteristics reflects the intricate beauty of divine artistry. These variations reflect God's creativity, emphasizing the complexity and magnificence of human life. Rather than fostering division, this diversity should promote unity, highlighting the splendor of God's creation.

CHAPTER 3
The Nature Of Angels

Some believers hold the view that God created man alone, but that is not true. Otherwise, the scriptures would not have used "us" in the book of Genesis, chapter 1, verse 26. God did not create man in isolation; He created man in consultation with His entire council, and this council is known as Elohim, a term that refers to the divine council or the congregation of the mighty ones. Notice what the scripture says:

"Then God said, 'Let us make mankind in our image, in our likeness, so that they may rule over the fish in the sea and the birds in the sky, over the livestock and all the wild animals, and over all the creatures that move along the ground.'"(Gen 1:26)

Just as every person has unique elemental associations, so too do the angels of God. Some angels are aligned with fire, others with air, water, or earth. Those attuned to the element of air belong to the cohort of Michael, while those associated with water are part of Gabriel's assembly. Angels linked to earth are members of Raphael's group, and those connected to fire belong to Uriel's family. Michael, Gabriel, Raphael, and Uriel are not individual angels but cohorts of angels, each with distinct elemental affiliations.

When we consider human nature, we recognize that each aspect of our being corresponds to specific angelic influences. The angel Michael is linked to the airy dimension of the human spirit. Gabriel, associated with the water element, pertains to the blood within us. Raphael is connected to the earthly aspect of humanity, while Uriel is linked with the fiery element within us. These angelic beings each fulfill unique and fascinating roles in the universe. For instance, Raphael and his companions specialize in healing.

The name Raphael, originating from the Hebrew "Rāfāʾēl" meaning "God heals" or "The mighty one who heals," aptly reflects his traditional role as a divine overseer of healing, encompassing illness, infirmity, and restoration. When God appoints ministers of God as healers, He sends Raphael to aid them in their ministry. Jesus was assigned Raphael, which accounts for the prominent role of healing in His ministry. The angel, who worked alongside Jesus from Raphael's family, was named Virtue. During one of His journeys to Jairus's house, a woman who had suffered from a bleeding condition for twelve years approached Jesus. The Scriptures recount that virtue departed from Him as soon as she touched Him, illustrating the divine power at work. While many interpret this virtue as a loss of strength, it was, in fact, an angel's Virtue who played a role in easing the woman's healing. Consider the words of Scripture:

> *"When she heard about Jesus, she came up behind him in the crowd and touched his cloak because she thought, 'If I just touch his clothes, I will be healed.' Immediately, her bleeding stopped, and she felt in her body that she was freed from her suffering. At once, Jesus realized that Virtue had gone out of him. He turned around in the crowd and asked, 'Who touched my clothes?' 'You see the people crowding against you,' his disciples answered, 'and yet you can ask, "Who touched me?"' But Jesus kept looking around to see who had done it. Then the woman, knowing what had happened to her, came and fell at his feet and, trembling with fear, told him the whole truth."*

(Mark 5:27-33, NIV)

THE RISE AND FALL OF LUCIFER

Many believers today mistakenly use the names Lucifer and Satan interchangeably, yet Scripture reveals that they are not the same. The name Lucifer, meaning "light-bringer" or "morning star," originates from the Latin translation of Isaiah 14:12, which declares, "How art thou fallen from heaven, O Lucifer, son of the morning!" This term is not inherently evil; in fact, it is etymologically related to words like "luminous," meaning "full of light." This is why names such as Lucy—the feminine form of Lucifer—are still used today without any negative spiritual connotation. Lucifer was a being of divine light, created in splendor, whose name reflected his radiant nature and exalted function. Before his fall, he was a magnificent and glorious creation of God, endowed with wisdom, beauty, and priestly authority. Ezekiel 28:13–14 vividly describes him: "Thou hast been in Eden the garden of God; every precious stone was thy covering... Thou art the anointed cherub that covereth; and I have set thee so." Lucifer wore a priestly garment adorned with nine precious stones, symbolizing his sacred office. More than just a celestial figure, Lucifer had stewardship over the sanctuaries in heaven, as confirmed in Ezekiel 28:18: "Thou hast defiled thy sanctuaries by the multitude of thine iniquities…" His role was both exalted and sacred—a high-ranking guardian of divine order within the heavenly realm. Lucifer's fall was not due to weakness but to pride and ambition. Driven by a desire to ascend above his station, he sought to exalt himself above the other archangels and ultimately above God Himself. As recorded in Isaiah 14:13, "For thou hast said in thine heart, I will ascend into heaven, I will exalt my throne above the stars of God: I will also sit upon the mount of the congregation…" Here, the "stars" represent the angels of God, a symbolism also affirmed in Revelation 1:20, where the stars are described as "the angels of the seven churches."

At that time, the heavenly hierarchy included four principal archangels, each governing a specific domain of creation: Michael, commander of the heavenly hosts, had authority over the air; Gabriel, the divine messenger, presided over the waters; Raphael, the healer, was charged with the earth; and Uriel, the fiery one, commanded fire. Lucifer, however, sought to usurp their domains and elevate himself above them. Yet these angels remained faithful to God's order and did not relinquish their authority. It was in the aftermath of this rebellion that Lucifer was cast out of heaven, and his identity was transformed. He became known as Satan, a name meaning "adversary" or "accuser," signaling his new role as the opposer of God's purposes and the deceiver of mankind. Satan is not who Lucifer was—but who he became. The radiant light-bearer descended into corruption, turning his light into darkness, yet still retaining his status as a being of light—albeit a perverted one. Both Lucifer and Satan are light beings by nature, but where Lucifer bore light to illuminate, Satan distorts that light to deceive. This transformation is not merely symbolic but carries eternal consequence. Revelation 20:1–3 foretells Satan's judgment: "And I saw an angel come down from heaven... and he laid hold on the dragon, that old serpent, which is the Devil, and Satan, and bound him a thousand years." He will be imprisoned in the bottomless pit for a millennium, only to be released "for a season" to deceive the nations once again (Revelation 20:7–8), leading to his final and eternal destruction. Understanding the distinction between Lucifer and Satan is essential for believers. Lucifer was once a glorious priest of heaven, entrusted with divine responsibility and radiating God's light. Satan is the fallen version of that being—a tragic corruption, the result of pride, rebellion, and the defilement of light.

CHAPTER 4
The Element Of The Earth

The Earth Signs: Zodiac Signs, Houses, and Career Paths.

Astrology intricately connects each zodiac sign to specific elements, houses, and inherent strengths, collectively shaping potential career paths. Taurus, Virgo, and Capricorn—the three Earth signs— do more than symbolize the Earth element; they serve as gateways to distinct vocational directions. Known for their practicality, dependability, and steadfastness, these signs are connected to specific houses within the astrological chart. This alignment significantly influences career inclinations and strengths, offering a clear perspective on how astrology can guide professional aspirations that resonate with the unique traits of each Earth sign.

Taurus: The Second House (House of Value)

Beginning with Taurus, the foremost Earth sign, this zodiac aligns with the 2nd House, often called the House of Value. This significant house governs personal finances, material possessions, and one's self-worth. Taureans epitomize practicality, reliability, patience, and a strong work ethic, making them well-suited for careers that demand stability and a systematic approach.

Virgo: The Sixth House (House of Health and Service)

Virgo, the second Earth sign, is associated with the 6th House, which focuses centrally on health, service, and daily routines. With their analytical prowess and meticulous nature, Virgos excel in roles requiring precision and dedication to service. Their service-oriented mindset and attention to detail align them perfectly with careers demanding analytical skills and commitment to serving others.

Capricorn: The Tenth House (House of Career and Public Standing)

Capricorn, the third Earth sign, is intricately linked with the 10th House, the House of Career and Public Standing. This pivotal house governs ambitions, career trajectories, and social status. Capricorns are renowned for their ambition, discipline, responsibility, and resourcefulness, which drive them toward leadership roles and success in structured environments. Their ability to keep focus on long-term goals make them inspiring figures in professional settings.

Summary Table

Zodiac Sign	House	Element	Career Paths
Taurus	2nd House (Value)	Earth	Finance, Real Estate, Culinary Arts, Agriculture, Art, Construction
Virgo	6th House (Health)	Earth	Healthcare, Research, Editing, Teaching, Administration, Environmental Science
Capricorn	10th House (Career)	Earth	Business, Law, Engineering, Architecture, Management, Accounting

As Earth signs, you bring unique qualities to the professional arena. Your ability to skillfully use your talents and strengths allows you to excel in careers that demand reliability, attention to detail, and practicality. Whether you are fostering financial stability, providing meticulous service, or assuming ambitious leadership roles, Taurus, Virgo, and Capricorn carve out distinctive vocational paths that align with your natural characteristics. Your steadfast approach and grounded nature ensure success in endeavors that require dedication, precision, and long-term vision, making you an invaluable asset in various professional fields.

The Earth as A Witness

Everything in creation has a spiritual counterpart that mirrors its physical form, revealing the deeper nature behind what we perceive with our senses. This truth, though foundational, is often overlooked, highlighting a gap in understanding. Consider the heavens, the seas, and the trees in the Garden of Eden—each element has a corresponding spiritual entity linked to it. The unseen spiritual dimension is deeply embedded in the fabric of creation, yet it often remains unnoticed or unacknowledged. Recognizing these spiritual counterparts enriches our understanding, opening a fascinating world of interconnectedness between the physical and spiritual realms.

Take, for example, the Tree of the Knowledge of Good and Evil in the Garden of Eden. Its spiritual counterpart was the serpent, which is clear in its interaction with Eve. The spiritual force behind the tree played a pivotal role in tempting humanity, leading to the fall. This is a powerful confirmation of the reality of spiritual entities influencing the physical world. In the African society where I was born and bred, stories abound of trees that have swallowed families' treasures, held women's wombs, or buried essential documents.

While such accounts may seem unbelievable or superstitious to some, they are deeply rooted in the belief that spiritual forces directly affect human experiences.

When biblical writers attribute human qualities to inanimate objects, they are not simply using symbolism but acknowledging spiritual realities. These descriptions illustrate the interconnectedness of the physical and spiritual realms, reminding us that there is often more than meets the eye. As believers, we must not dismiss these accounts as mere allegories but recognize them as reflections of spiritual truths. Understanding the spiritual dimension of creation is enriching and empowering as it deepens our comprehension of God's sovereignty and the complex relationship between the seen and the unseen worlds.

Indeed, just as elements like water, heaven, and trees have spiritual beings associated with them, the earth also has a spirit connected to it, and this spirit is feminine. The earth is often referred to with feminine attributes in scripture, and explicit scriptural references support this notion.

Firstly, the Bible explicitly says that the earth can write, implying the presence of hands. In Jeremiah 22:30 (KJV), it is written: ***"Thus saith the LORD, write ye this man childless, a man that shall not prosper in his days: for no man of his seed shall prosper, sitting upon the throne of David, and ruling any more in Judah."***

Secondly, the earth is depicted as having a hearing ability akin to that of humans or animals. Jeremiah 22:29 (KJV) reinforces this idea: ***"O earth, earth, earth, hear the word of the LORD."***

Thirdly, the earth is described as having the ability to swallow with her mouth, as indicated in Numbers 16:30: "But if the LORD make a new thing, and the earth open her mouth, and swallow them up, with all that appertain unto them, and they go down quick into the pit; then ye shall understand that these men have provoked the LORD."

Lastly, the earth is described as having the ability to help just like any other human being. Revelation 12:16 (KJV) illustrates this: ***"And the earth helped the woman, and the earth opened her mouth, and swallowed up the flood which the dragon cast out of his mouth."*** This passage not only portrays the earth as a sentient being capable of aiding others, but it also underscores the idea that the earth, like all of God's creation, is part of a more extensive interconnected system. Just as the earth aided the woman in this biblical narrative, it continually sustains and supports life every day, providing the foundation for growth, nourishment, and vitality. According to the scriptures above, the earth is described with anthropomorphic features, such as eyes, a mouth, hands, and even a womb. These descriptions provide a literal portrayal, affirming the earth's identity as a feminine persona.

In the Akan dialect, the name "**earth**" reveals its feminine nature as "Asaase Yaa." In Akan, "Asaase" means land, and "Yaa" refers to a female born on Thursday. This linguistic insight does not imply the Earth was born on a Thursday but confirms its feminine identity. Like many other cultures, the Akan people personify the earth as a nurturing and life-giving entity, hence the feminine association. If there is any doubt that the Earth is feminine, consider why we refer to her as our motherland. The physical earth has a spiritual counterpart, represented as a woman. Like us, she experiences emotions and mood swings based on how she is treated.

For instance, if you disobey and ridicule authority like parents, clergymen, gods, etc., the earth will open her belly and swallow you. Some people have suffered premature death simply because they defied authority figures. This is not to say that the earth is a vengeful entity, but rather to illustrate the spiritual principle that our actions have consequences. On the contrary, if you revere authority and preserve the earth and all of God's creation, the earth will yield strength for you. Please do not underestimate the earth; she can either nurture your prosperity or destroy you.

The Woman and The Serpent

In the Revelation of Jesus Christ, an intense conflict unfolds between an audacious woman and the serpent, each drawing upon their respective elemental forces. This confrontation, detailed in the scripture, highlights the pivotal role that these elemental attributes play in the cosmic struggle. The passage from Revelation 12:13-16 recounts:

> *"And when the dragon saw that he was cast unto the earth, he persecuted the woman, who brought forth the man's child. And to the woman were given two wings of a great eagle, that she might fly into the wilderness, into her place, where she is nourished for a time and times, and half a time, from the face of the serpent. And the serpent cast out of his mouth water as a flood after the woman, so that he might cause her to be carried away by the flood. And the earth helped the woman, and the earth opened her mouth, and swallowed up the flood the dragon cast out of his mouth."*

(Revelation 12:13-16, KJV)

In this passage, Scorpio—represented by the serpent—unleashes a flood as a manifestation of its elemental power: water. As a water sign, Scorpio channels emotional intensity and transformative energy through this element, using it here as a weapon to overwhelm the woman. However, the woman symbolizes Virgo, whose elemental nature is Earth—steady, grounded, and resilient. When the flood is released, the Earth intervenes on her behalf, opening to absorb the waters and neutralize the serpent's attack. Why does the Earth come to her aid? The Earth protects her because it is her elemental counterpart—an intrinsic part of her being. This vivid interaction draws on ancient archetypes, echoing the primordial struggle in the Garden of Eden.There, Eve—who embodies Virgo—faced the serpent, the very manifestation of Scorpio.In both narratives, the opposition between the woman and the serpent is not merely symbolic; it is elemental. The water of the serpent (Scorpio) clashes with the earth of the woman (Virgo), representing an underlying discord in their fundamental natures. This elemental conflict serves as a metaphor for human relationships. When individuals form bonds—particularly romantic or marital ones—without understanding the nature of their elemental affinities, tension can arise. For instance, when someone aligned with the Earth element (practical, stable, grounded) joins with someone of the Water element (emotional, fluid, deep), their differing energies may create ongoing friction. Earth seeks structure and reliability, while Water craves emotional depth and transformation. Without awareness and balance, these divergent energies may struggle to coexist, often leading to conflict, emotional distance, or even separation. The cosmic tension between Virgo and Scorpio thus mirrors the challenges faced in real-life relationships when elemental energies are incompatible. Just as the Earth rose to defend the woman in the biblical vision and stood firm against the chaos symbolized by the serpent, so too can understanding one's elemental nature provide protection and insight. By aligning with a partner whose elemental energy complements your own, you foster harmony, mutual support, and long-term balance.

Ultimately, knowing your elemental affiliation—whether Earth, Water, Fire, or Air—offers profound wisdom in navigating relationships. It allows you to choose connections that align naturally with your essence, avoiding unnecessary discord and nurturing bonds that thrive in elemental harmony.

The Earth as A Witness of Prayer

God created the earth and made it a neutral or beggarly element.

Notice what the scripture says:

"The earth is the LORD's, and the fullness thereof; the world, and they that dwell therein. For he hath founded it upon the seas and established it upon the floods."

(Psalms 24:1-2, KJV).

Since the earth is neutral, anyone, good or evil, can use it to their advantage. Traditionalists, Muslims, Christians, Jews, and others can use the earth to perpetuate either evil or good. Besides being a neutral entity, the Earth also serves as a witness. The universe has many witnesses, and the Earth is one of them. Notice what the scripture says:

"I call heaven and earth to witness against you this day, that ye shall soon utterly perish from off the land whereunto ye go over Jordan to possess it; ye shall not prolong your days upon it but shall utterly be destroyed."

(Deuteronomy 4:26, KJV).

Like every human, the earth has the faculties to listen, plead cases, and record petitions, as she has physical attributes enabling her to hear, write, and speak. Engaging the elements of the universe in prayer is scriptural. Scripture affirms this practice:

"And it shall come to pass in that day, I will hear, saith the LORD, I will hear the heavens, and they shall hear the earth, and the earth shall hear the corn, and the wine, and the oil; and they shall hear Jezreel."

(Hosea 2:21-23, KJV).

Have you wondered why fetish priests and priestesses use oil, schnapps, the earth, and other elements to pray? It is because they understand the modus operandi of prayer. They know how to engage the elements for their prayers to be answered, yet many believers are clueless about engaging them to their advantage. Why do some believers secretly go and seek help from these fetish priests and priestesses when they need the fruit of the womb, breakthroughs, financial elevation, and so on? The truth is that they believe their requests can be granted faster than when they resort to the traditional Christian route of prayer. Most believers get frustrated the more they pray because they do not know how to engage God's divine providence in prayer. Prayer becomes futile and frustrating when it is done without understanding.

Understanding the principles of prayer and how to engage with the elements of God's creation can enhance its effectiveness. This is not to suggest turning away from God but rather to deepen one's understanding of the tools God has provided within creation to aid in prayer. Merely invoking the name of Jesus in prayer is not enough; the name of Jesus and the other provisions of God must be actively engaged together to work for your benefit.

Manipulation Of the Element of The Earth

The earth is one of the elements that the enemy seeks to exploit to harm lives, and as believers, the onus is on us to guard ourselves against its destructive influence. One such element that the enemy manipulates is dust, which attaches to our footprints. Dust is often linked to a curse, and poverty typically follows wherever it is present. The dust in your environment can contribute to poverty, so it is essential to keep your surroundings free from dust to overcome poverty. Consider what the scripture says in 1 Samuel 2:8 (KJV):

"He raiseth up the poor out of the dust, and lifteth up the beggar from the dunghill, to set them among princes, and to make them inherit the throne of glory: for the pillars of the earth are the LORD's, and he hath set the world upon them."

According to this scripture, dust is depicted as an element of the earth that perpetuates poverty. If dust stays on one's feet, the spirit of poverty may persist in that person's life. Have you ever dreamt of being stuck in mud or a dusty environment? Such dreams are often symbolic of poverty and an inability to succeed. The remedy for overcoming this issue is foot washing. Jesus Himself instituted foot washing, and any believer who ridicules this practice is ignorant of its significance.

Furthermore, those who still doubt that dust is the root cause of poverty should consider comparing dust-free regions with dusty ones. Countries, cities, and provinces in Europe and America that have successfully eradicated dust from their environments have prospered. In contrast, areas that have not addressed dust-related issues are still impoverished. This stark difference shows the impact of dust on socioeconomic conditions.

Additionally, one of the technologies that the enemy uses to destroy the destinies of believers is their footprints or the dust on their feet. Why does the enemy use your footprint? Your footprint holds information about your destiny. Just as your fingerprint can verify your identity, your footprint can also be used to gather personal information. Many believers' destinies have been jeopardized because the enemy accessed their footprints. How did Satan destroy Job and all his possessions? It was through his footprint. Notice what the scripture says in Job 13:27 (KJV):

"Thou puttest my feet also in the stocks, and lookest narrowly unto all my paths; thou settest a print upon the heels of my feet."

The enemy traces our footprints, collects the dust from our feet, and uses it against us. Satan's attacks are not always physical; often, he exploits our vulnerabilities through subtle means, such as manipulating our footprints. How can you tell if the enemy has used your footprint against you? When medical professionals cannot provide solutions for your illnesses, it may indicate your footprint has been tampered with. In such cases, spiritual steps must be taken to address the issue.

Have you ever wondered why God's feet are never tampered with? It is because His feet are untraceable and beyond the enemy's reach. Psalms 77:19 (KJV) states:

"Thy way is in the sea, and thy path in the great waters, and thy footsteps are unknown."

Since our feet are traceable, we must constantly safeguard them by washing them with water or other means to protect ourselves spiritually.

CHAPTER 5
The Element Of The Air

Astrologically, the zodiac signs associated with the air element—Gemini, Libra, and Aquarius—are characterized by intelligence, effective communication skills, and adaptability, enabling them to thrive in various professional fields.

Gemini, represented by the Twins, embodies versatility and intellectual curiosity. People born under this sign are natural communicators, adept at articulating ideas clearly and engaging diverse audiences. Their ability to quickly absorb and process information makes them excel in journalism, writing, public relations, broadcasting, and sales careers. The air element empowers them to navigate dynamic environments, fostering the innovation and flexibility necessary for success.

Libra, symbolized by the Scales, is balance, diplomacy, and fairness. Libras excel in professions requiring negotiation, mediation, creativity, and ethical judgment. Whether as lawyers, diplomats, counsellors, artists, or designers, they use their air element to promote harmony and resolve conflicts with tact and diplomacy. Their effective communication capabilities allow them to easily analyze complex situations, cultivating collaborative environments where consensus-building and teamwork are essential.

Aquarius, symbolized by the Water Bearer, is known for its independence, innovation, and humanitarianism. Aquarians are celebrated for their forward-thinking, progressive ideas. They thrive in careers focused on innovation, intellectual pursuits, and social change, such as science, invention, social activism, technology, and community organizing. Their air element fuels their ability to challenge norms, envision new possibilities, and advocate for transformative ideas. Analytical thinking and problem-solving skills help them embrace technological advancements, driving progress across industries and society.

The elemental advantage of air signs lies in their communication skills, intellectual curiosity, and adaptability. Excelling in conveying ideas effectively, negotiating skillfully, and building robust networks, Geminis, Libras, and Aquarians are equipped to thrive in diverse environments. Their innate curiosity propels them to gather and critically analyze information, aiding informed decision-making. Moreover, their adaptability allows them to embrace change with agility, navigate challenges, and seize growth opportunities. Geminis, Libras, and Aquarians can maximise their potential across their chosen career paths by harnessing their air element strengths. Their contributions drive personal success and enrich professional landscapes with innovation, ethical leadership, and a commitment to positive societal impact. By understanding the nuances of their elemental affinity, these individuals can confidently advance, making significant strides in their professional growth and positively affecting their fields.

The Holy Spirit

When you thoroughly study the Holy Scriptures, you will discover a divine personality associated with the air: The Holy Spirit. Just as every individual is assigned a guardian angel, the Holy Spirit serves as the guardian angel of our Lord Jesus Christ. Within the Trinity, He is a distinct person endowed with intellect, emotions, and the ability to convey the mysteries of God to the churches. The Holy Spirit acts as a messenger and the earthly presence of Jesus Christ, embodying the spirit of our Heavenly Father and playing a vital role within the Godhead. As an ethereal being, the Holy Spirit fulfils diverse functions and has a unique ministry to believers and the Church. He serves as a helper and comforter, faithfully fulfilling His role as outlined in scripture:

"But the Comforter, which is the Holy Ghost, whom the Father will send in my name, he shall teach you all things, and bring all things to your remembrance, whatsoever I have said unto you."

(John 14:26, KJV)

The primary mission of the Holy Spirit is to teach and reveal the intentions of the Father to His children. When a believer is unable to hear from the Holy Spirit, it signals a form of spiritual deafness that requires urgent attention. The Holy Spirit speaks in several ways—through dreams, visions, and other divine impressions. However, when one is unable to recognize or understand these streams of communication, they risk missing the voice of God and the guidance it brings.

Unfortunately, many churches today experience stagnation in spiritual growth and maturity because their leaders lack spiritual sensitivity. One of the prevailing spiritual conditions affecting many church leaders is both spiritual blindness and deafness—conditions that leave them unable to perceive or respond to the voice of God. As a result, they are often incapable of discerning and communicating the divine truths and mysteries that are essential for the transformation and development of believers. Scripture repeatedly emphasizes the necessity of spiritual awareness. In Revelation 2:7 (KJV), it is written: *"He that hath an ear, let him hear what the Spirit saith unto the churches."* This call is not merely about physical hearing but about spiritual receptivity—the ability to discern the voice of the Holy Spirit and respond in obedience. When leaders are spiritually deaf, they miss the audible voice of God—the direct, prompt communication meant to guide the Church. Without this divine insight, they cannot decode the mysteries of God, and the people under their care remain spiritually malnourished. True growth in the body of Christ requires leaders who can hear clearly from the Spirit, rightly divide the word of truth, and lead others into deeper understanding and alignment with God's will.

Just as air itself is invisible to the naked eye while its effects are clearly perceptible, so too does the Holy Spirit's presence reveal itself through tangible traits and transformative experiences in the lives of believers. Living without the Holy Spirit equates to an incomplete Christian journey. While some believers are naturally born with the Holy Spirit, others must consciously believe and receive Him as a gift from our Heavenly Father. The importance of the Holy Spirit cannot be overemphasised, and every believer must actively walk in communion with Him.

CHAPTER 6
The Element Of Fire

The zodiac fire signs—Aries, Leo, and Sagittarius—each have distinct qualities that make them natural leaders and pioneers in their chosen fields. With their innate drive, creativity, and enthusiasm, these signs excel in roles that require bold action, innovation, and the ability to inspire others. Comprehending the unique traits of Aries, Leo, and Sagittarius can offer valuable insight into how these elemental energies can be harnessed for professional success.

As an Aries, the first sign of the zodiac, they are ruled by Mars and symbolize courage, initiative, and enthusiasm. They are known for their dynamic energy, leadership qualities, and competitive spirit. Professionally, they thrive in careers that offer excitement and the opportunity to take charge. They excel in roles such as entrepreneur, military officer, athlete, or emergency responder. The key to their success lies in harnessing their natural drive and fearlessness, setting clear goals, and focusing on achieving them. However, they must learn to manage their impatience and impulsiveness by developing strategic thinking and patience to reach their highest potential.

Transitioning to Leo, the fifth sign of the zodiac, individuals shift from raw, impulsive action to a more refined and charismatic expression of leadership. Ruled by the Sun, Leo embodies creativity, confidence, and leadership. They are known for their charismatic personality, generosity, and flair for the dramatic. They shine in careers that allow them to be in the spotlight and express their creativity. Ideal professions for them include acting, sports, politics, and event planning. They must use their natural charm and leadership skills to achieve their career goals while learning to collaborate effectively with others and manage their ego. Continuous self-improvement and humility can help them gain the respect and support of their peers, paving the way for long-term success.

Finally, as Sagittarius, the ninth sign of the zodiac, they are ruled by Jupiter and embody adventure, optimism, and a quest for knowledge. They are known for their love of freedom, philosophical outlook, and enthusiasm for exploring new horizons. They excel in careers with variety, intellectual stimulation, and travel opportunities. Their suitable professions include travel writer, professor, explorer, and motivational speaker. To succeed, they must focus on setting achievable goals and maintaining discipline. While their adventurous spirit is a great asset, they must also learn to balance it with practicality and follow through on their commitments.

Despite their distinct traits, Aries, Leo, and Sagittarius all share the common element of fire, which fuels their passion, ambition, and dynamic energy. This shared elemental connection expresses how fire signs can uniquely channel their energy to achieve their professional aspirations. From Aries' impulsive action to Leo's charismatic leadership and Sagittarius' expansive pursuit of knowledge and adventure, we see a natural progression in how fire signs use their elemental drive to propel themselves forward in various fields. Individuals with fire signs should fully embrace their natural enthusiasm, creativity, and leadership qualities to harness their career potential. However, they must address challenges such as impulsiveness, egocentrism, and the tendency to overextend themselves by taking on too many projects. Cultivating self-awareness and emotional intelligence will allow them to navigate their professional landscape more easily. Practical strategies, such as setting clear priorities, seeking constructive feedback, and committing to continuous learning, can help them stay grounded and remain focused on their goals.

The Fiery Nature Of A Man

The concept of the soul as a fiery essence within everyone is deeply rooted in the Word of God. It is the core connection to the unseen dimensions of existence, shaping one's interaction with the spiritual realm. In certain Christian circles, this is referred to as the "**third eye.**" When the soul is vibrant and alive, it eases spiritual experiences, such as the ability to dream during sleep. Dreams are not random occurrences but serve as conduits through which the soul conveys insights, warnings, and guidance to the conscious mind.

At times, you may struggle to dream while asleep. This often indicates that the fire within you—the soul—has been quenched. Such a spiritual condition disrupts your connection to the spiritual realm, preventing you from receiving messages via dreams. Many people experience this phenomenon due to a lack of vitality in their souls.

Recognizing this state is essential, as it calls for intentional efforts to rekindle and restore the inner fire. Dreaming allows the soul to move beyond the physical realm, opening the door to divine revelations and insights. When you are unable to dream or recall your dreams, it may signify spiritual disconnection or intoxication. Just as excessive wine clouds the mind and memory, spiritual intoxication can cloud your awareness and hinder your ability to experience and recall dreams.

Ephesians 5:18 admonishes, "*Do not drink wine, which leads to debauchery. Instead, be filled with the Spirit*." This verse emphasizes the importance of maintaining spiritual clarity and sobriety. If you are struggling with dreaming or recollecting your dreams, it may suggest the need to awaken the senses of your soul. In such cases, seeking guidance from a genuine man of God can help rekindle the fire within you and restore your ability to receive divine messages via dreams.

The fiery essence of the soul is not merely symbolic but a foundational aspect of human nature. It is a transformative force that influences one's engagement with the spiritual realm. Paying attention to dreams and seeking spiritual clarity is essential for those aspiring to achieve a deeper understanding of the divine and gain insight into life's unfolding events. This spiritual fire can inspire and bring hope, transforming our lives and guiding us toward a deeper connection with God.

Baptism Of Fire: The Believer's Experience

Besides the innate fire within every person, there is a specific fire that a believer can be baptized with and that fire is popularly known as 'holy fire.' This holy fire is not a literal flame but a spiritual manifestation of God's presence and power. When baptized with the Holy Spirit, believers are filled with this holy fire, which ignites their faith and empowers them for spiritual service. Every believer is expected to undergo various baptismal experiences, and fire baptism is no exception. Why place so much emphasis on water baptism? Is that the only baptismal experience a believer must undergo? Certainly not! Jesus clearly stated, in contrast to John the Baptist, that He came to baptize with the Holy Spirit and fire.

> *"John answered them all, 'I baptise you with water. But one who is more powerful than I will come, the straps of whose sandals I am not worthy to untie. He will baptise you with the Holy Spirit and fire."*

(Luke 3:16, NIV)

The importance of fire baptism is immense. Just as a clinical thermometer assesses a person's physical temperature, every believer must constantly evaluate their spiritual temperature. The Bible offers clear guidance on maintaining this spiritual warmth. It is not a passive process but an active one that requires our attention and effort. The Bible speaks clearly about spiritual temperature:

> *"I know your deeds, that you are neither cold nor hot. I wish you were either one or the other! So, because you are lukewarm—neither hot nor cold—I am about to spit you out of my mouth." This verse underscores the need for spiritual warmth, for it is this warmth that fuels our motivation and commitment to our faith.*

(Revelation 3:15-16, NIV)

How do you measure the fire within you? By the word of God. Just as a clinical thermometer measures body temperature, the word of God measures your spiritual temperature. If you hear the word of God and are unwilling to go the extra mile to spread it, then you are cold. Conversely, if you eagerly share the word you have received, you are hot:

> *"They got up and returned at once to Jerusalem. There they found the Eleven and those with them, assembled and saying, 'It is true! The Lord has risen and has appeared to Simon.' Then the two told what had happened on the way and how they recognised Jesus when he broke the bread."*

(Luke 24:33-35, NIV)

In Luke 24:33-35, the passage describes the encounter of two disciples with Jesus on the road to Emmaus. These disciples discussed recent events concerning Jesus' crucifixion and the reports of his resurrection. Along the way, they were joined by a stranger who, unbeknownst to them, was Jesus himself. They talked about the scriptures, and upon reaching Emmaus, they invited the stranger to stay with them for the evening meal. During the meal, Jesus took the bread, blessed it, broke it, and gave it to them, which was a moment of revelation for the disciples. As He broke the bread, their eyes were opened, and they recognized Him. However, at that instant, Jesus disappeared from their sight. Filled with joy and amazement, they returned to Jerusalem, where they found the Eleven apostles gathered with others. They shared their story of meeting Jesus on the road and how they recognized Him when He broke the bread.

This passage is significant as it accentuates Jesus' post-resurrection appearances and his ongoing presence with his disciples. It emphasizes the transformative power of encountering Jesus, primarily through breaking bread, reminiscent of the Last Supper. The disciples' journey to Emmaus and their later return to Jerusalem with the news of Jesus' appearance further solidified the reality of the resurrection. It strengthened the faith of the early believers and stands as a testament to Jesus' promise to be with His followers always, even after His physical departure from earth. The love that compelled them to go the extra mile in spreading the message of Jesus was born from a fire ignited within them. Love is often the driving force, intricately linked to fire and inseparable from its essence. If you lack enthusiasm for the Word of God and are unwilling to fulfil the commandment of love, you are spiritually cold and need your inner fire reignited. Jesus warned about the state of spiritual coldness in the last days:

"And because lawlessness will abound, the love of many will grow cold."

(Matthew 24:12, NKJV)

It is common to see individuals who were once passionate and vibrant in their Christian faith during their time in universities and colleges, only to disappear later or even become antagonistic toward the church. What leads people to grow spiritually cold? Often, it is the influence of negative associations and an increasing focus on self-interest. To keep spiritual vibrancy, it is essential to surround yourself with others who share your zeal for Christ. Conversely, if you stay fervent but immerse yourself in an environment of spiritually indifferent or cold believers, such as those who show little interest in spiritual matters or are more focused on material wealth, you risk becoming lukewarm. The environment you choose plays a significant role in shaping your spiritual condition.

Furthermore, spiritual coldness often arises from a self-centered mindset, where one's focus narrows to personal welfare, the immediate family, and personal concerns. This inward focus prevents individuals from stepping outside their comfort zones to engage with and serve those in need, and in doing so, they become disconnected from the broader work of God's kingdom.

Undergoing baptism with the Holy Spirit and fire is crucial for every believer. It empowers you, reignites your love for God, and strengthens your commitment to spreading the gospel. By assessing your spiritual state through God's Word and surrounding yourself with genuine believers, you can keep or rekindle the fire within, enabling you to fulfill your purpose in Christ with passion and dedication.

The Fiery Angels

The term "Seraphim" derives from the Hebrew word "seraph," meaning "burning ones" or "fiery ones," with the suffix "im" indicating the plural form. This name is rooted in a specific biblical passage in Isaiah 6:2-3 (NIV):

"In the year that King Uzziah died, I saw the Lord, high and exalted, seated on a throne, and the train of His robe filled the temple. Above Him were seraphim, each with six wings: With two wings, they covered their faces; with two, they covered their feet; and with two, they were flying. And they were calling to one another: 'Holy, holy, holy is the Lord Almighty; the whole earth is full of His glory.'"

In this vision, Isaiah is granted a glimpse of the heavenly throne room, where seraphim surround God's exalted presence. These angelic beings are described with six wings: two covering their faces, two covering their feet, and two for flight. The seraphim's fundamental role is the continuous worship and adoration of God, constantly declaring His holiness. Their "burning" nature symbolizes their radiant purity and intense devotion, as their essence is aflame with a zeal for God.

The imagery of covering their faces and feet underscores the reverence and awe they feel in God's presence, their humility, and submission. The two wings used for flight represent their readiness to carry out divine will with speed and obedience. Positioned around God's throne, the seraphim are charged with keeping the sanctity of the divine presence, serving as eternal guardians of the heavenly realm.

In their divine role, the seraphim also oversee altars across the universe, godly and ungodly. These altars, meticulously recorded by the seraphim, hold a profound spiritual importance as they serve as the meeting points of the divine and earthly realms. The seraphim's presence at these altars reminds believers of the need for fervent spirituality and sincere devotion to God, underscoring the importance of purity and dedication in every aspect of life.

The Token of Salt

The connection between salt and fire is deeply embedded in Scripture, carrying spiritual significance throughout the Bible. In Mark 9:49-50, Jesus conveys this truth:

"You will be salted with fire. Salt is good, but if it loses its saltiness, how can you restore its flavor? Have salt within yourselves and live in peace with one another."

In this passage, Jesus emphasizes the connection between salt and fire, underscoring their lasting spiritual significance. Like wine and bread symbolize Christ's body and blood, salt, strongly associated with fire, holds equal importance in Christianity. It stands for purification, preservation, and enhancement, functioning in both the physical and spiritual realms. This spiritual aspect of salt is further expressed in Colossians 4:6: "*Let your conversation be always full of grace, seasoned with salt, so you may know how to answer everyone.*"

This verse encourages us to season our words with salt, bringing wisdom and grace to our interactions with others. It calls for com-communication that positively influences and uplifts those we engage with. In prophetic ministry, salt is often used as a tool for spiritual direction. Those who are spiritually discerning recognize its importance and apply it with care. When a genuine prophet directs the use of salt in a prophetic context, it is prudent to follow this direction, as salt offers valuable spiritual benefits. Practically, salt is used in sacrifices for atonement and consecration. To disregard salt as a means of deliverance, fortification, and preservation is to ignore its spiritual significance. While believers are called "the salt of the earth," we must still be seasoned with salt, as the Word of God instructs, ensuring that our lives reflect His wisdom and grace.

Fiery Ministers of The Gospel

One essential quality for those who minister to the Lord Jesus Christ is the presence of holy fire. As Scripture affirms in Psalms, *'He makes His ministers a flame of fire'* (Psalm 104:4, ESV) Recognizing this fire is essential in discerning true ministers of God. Have you ever encountered pastors, clergy, or prophets who lack this fervor? Such a deficiency may indicate that they are not fully embracing the roles they profess to hold.

How can you tell if you lack God's fire as a gospel minister? A clear sign is when your words, spoken in preaching or teaching, do not ignite passion in the hearts of your listeners. If your message does not stir them to action or move them emotionally, it shows a lack of the Holy Spirit's fire. The fire of the Holy Spirit, when present, has a transformative power, igniting passion and inspiring action. Jesus Christ Himself was baptized with fire, empowering His disciples to live out His teachings with zeal.

The fire in this context is not merely a fleeting emotional response from hearing the Word. It is a deep, inner drive that compels you to go beyond the ordinary for Christ. It should raise concern if congregants appear disengaged, fall asleep, or yawn during a sermon. This suggests that the minister lacks God's holy fire, or their passion has waned. In contrast, a fiery minister sparks a sense of urgency and commitment in their listeners, motivating them to pursue their faith with all their hearts. Jeremiah described God's Word as "*a fire in my bones*" (Jeremiah 20:9, ESV), reflecting the intense conviction and passion it ignited within him. Likewise, the Word of God should burn within the hearts of ministers, driving them to proclaim with enthusiasm and sincerity. Believers should seek leaders whose words are driven by a deep spiritual hunger; as such, ministers inspire active faith and wholehearted devotion.

Therefore, it is crucial to avoid churches where ministers lack this divine fire. Spiritual coldness can subtly spread throughout the congregation, diminishing zeal and weakening commitment. Instead, seek out ministers whose words are infused with the power and passion of the Holy Spirit. Such leaders will inspire greater devotion, reignite your faith, and guide you toward a life of vibrant spiritual fulfillment.

CHAPTER 7
The Element Of Water

In theological terms, the zodiac signs aligned with the water element—Cancer, Scorpio, and Pisces—represent the spiritual qualities of compassion, intensity, and creativity, respectively. These qualities shape their personalities and professional paths, reflecting the divine attributes of God's love, determination, and creativity.

If you identify with **Cancer**, your deep resonance with compassion, nurturing, and intuition traits reflects the divine call to care for others. Whether you comfort patients in a hospital, guide young minds in a classroom, or provide support in therapy sessions, your intuitive understanding of people's emotions and needs manifests God's love and empathy in your chosen profession.

As a **Scorpio**, your character is defined by intensity, determination, and emotional depth. You have a keen insight into human psychology and are drawn to careers where you can uncover mysteries and understand complex motivations. Professions in psychology, psychiatry, investigative journalism, or research align perfectly with your analytical mind and investigative nature. Your ability to focus intensely on unravelling hidden truths positions you for success in fields such as detective work or forensic science. Whether conducting research to address societal issues or delving into criminal investigations, your strategic analysis and profound understanding are crucial in making significant discoveries and bringing clarity to situations.

Pisces individuals are characterized by their creativity, empathy, and deep emotional connections, which shape their career paths. You thrive in careers within the arts—whether through music, dance, writing, or visual arts—where you can express your emotions and connect with others. Your compassionate nature also suits you for healing professions such as nursing, holistic therapies, or spiritual counselling. In these roles, your intuitive comprehension and analysis of human emotions and spiritual insights allow you to offer comfort and healing to those in need. Whether you are composing music that resonates with the soul, guiding individuals on their journey to wellness, or offering spiritual guidance, your ability to tap into deep emotional currents enriches your work and the lives you touch.

Understanding these water signs' strengths and career paths offers a powerful insight into how their elemental affinity influences their vocational choices and societal contributions. By embracing your innate qualities associated with the water element, you can con- confidently navigate your professional path with clarity and purpose. Whether you find fulfilment in caregiving, investigative fields, the arts, or healing professions, your emotional intelligence and intuitive insights empower you to make meaningful contributions aligned with your natural strengths. Embrace these traits as valuable assets that enable you to thrive in your chosen field and positively affect the world around you. The understanding and embracing of your elemental affinities are not just crucial but also empowering for personal growth and effective ministry.

CHAPTER 8
Purification Of Our Works

The Greek term "**pur**," derived from "purification," refers to fire. In mining, fire is used to purify gold and other substances, removing impurities to increase their purity. Fire also serves to test the quality of products. For example, gold is measured in carats, and while 24-carat gold may still have some impurities, it is purer than 22-carat gold because it has undergone a more thorough refining process with fire. The term "pure" does not suggest the complete elimination of impurities; rather, it denotes a product refined by fire, effectively removing or reducing impurities to a greater extent than if it had not undergone such a purification process. Similarly, God will test our works in the lake of fire to assess their quality. Scripture states, "*Each one's work will be made manifest, for the Day will disclose it, because it will be revealed by fire, and the fire will test what sort of work each one has done*" (1 Corinthians 3:13, ESV). This divine examination looks to reveal our works' true nature and integrity.

Our works will be scrutinized as fire refines gold to determine their value and authenticity. As 1 Corinthians 3:13 (KJV) says, "*Every man's work shall be made manifest: for the day shall declare it, because it shall be revealed by fire; and the fire shall try every man's work of what sort it is.*" The phrase "what sort it is" refers to the quality of our work. God will test the works of all people, not just Christians, but individuals from various faiths—Muslims, Buddhists, Hindus, atheists, and others. After the fire reveals the quality of our work, we will receive our rewards. This process calls for a profound reflection and understanding of our work, fostering a sense of introspection and contemplation.

Many believers will have their spirits saved on the Day of Judgment, yet their works may not endure the refining fire, meaning they will not receive the rewards they had hoped for. God is concerned not just with the quantity but also with the quality of our work. Simply doing good works is not enough; these works must endure the test of fire to be rewarded. Many Christians pride themselves on their accomplishments: winning thousands of souls, building churches, traveling the world to spread the gospel, and setting up orphanages. However, the key question remains: What will the quality of these works be when subjected to fire? It is commendable to prophesy, perform miracles, heal the sick, and engage in charitable deeds. However, it is essential to ask whether these works align with the standard set by Christ. Fulfilling those standards will help in seeking God's pleasure in a real sense.

If we do not assess the present judgment of our works, we risk carrying out God's tasks haphazardly and losing our eternal rewards. This is not meant to discourage us from undertaking great works for God, but to emphasize that these works must align with His will. We must listen attentively to His voice and observe His works to align ourselves with Him and collaborate effectively. By aligning our actions with God's instructions, we ensure that our works are both abundant and of high quality, able to endure the test of fire and earn us eternal rewards. This alignment provides us with all the required guidance and reassurance in our spiritual journey.

CHAPTER 9
The Elements And Their Corresponding Household Characteristics

Human beings are composed of four fundamental elements—fire, earth, air, and water—that define our physical composition and influence our personalities and inclinations. When individuals say they are "in their element," they acknowledge an alignment with one of these forces, each imbuing us with distinct traits and preferences.

Fire symbolizes passion, energy, and creativity, drawing individuals toward the kitchen. In this fiery domain, flavours converge, senses ignite, and hospitality flourishes. For those aligned with fire, the kitchen becomes more than a space for cooking—it is a place to channel intensity into culinary creations, nurturing others through food.

Earth embodies practicality and nurturing. Those resonating with this element find solace in the bedroom, a sanctuary for rest and rejuvenation. Surrounded by earthy tones and textures, they recharge their energies and find comfort. The bedroom reflects their stable and nurturing nature, where peace and security are cultivated.

Air signifies adaptability, intellect, and social interaction. Those aligned with air thrive in the living room, a dynamic space where ideas take flight, conversations flow, and creativity blossoms. It is a canvas for expression and fosters intellectual exchange, making it the ideal environment for air individuals.

Water represents reflection, intuition, and empathy. Those influenced by this element gravitate toward the bathroom, a serene oasis for cleansing and renewal. Amid soothing waters and tranquil surroundings, they experience emotional release and spiritual replenishment. For water-aligned individuals, the bathroom serves as a retreat where they cleanse both physically and emotionally.

The concept of elemental resonance, or the idea that individuals are naturally drawn to spaces that align with their elemental nature, provides insight into why individuals may feel varying affinities towards specific spaces in their homes. For example, someone whose elemental nature does not align with fire may not find the kitchen—a space often associated with creativity and energy—appealing. The bustling atmosphere may not resonate with their preferences, leaving them less inspired in that environment.

Conversely, those aligned with water may find deep solace in the bathroom, known for its calming ambiance and cleansing rituals. On the other hand, those whose elemental makeup does not favour water may not prioritize these practices or feel at ease in this space. Understanding and aligning your personal spaces with your elemental affinities can significantly promote your comfort and well-being, making your home a more nurturing, supportive and secure place to live in.

Air-aligned individuals who excel in communication and social interactions are drawn to the living room, where vibrant conversations and intellectual exchanges thrive. However, those less inclined to air may find the liveliness overwhelming, preferring quieter, more reflective spaces for deeper contemplation and reflections.

Earth individuals, grounded in stability and practicality, seek nurturing, secure environments. Their homes reflect this desire for routine and familiarity, offering a haven where they can cultivate stability and comfort.

Understanding elemental inclinations offers profound insight into emotional and psychological needs beyond simple physical preferences. By acknowledging these tendencies, individuals can create living spaces that support their well-being, enhance self-awareness, and foster deeper connections with others. This awareness also explains why some people feel drawn to or distant from some regions of the home. Aligning living spaces with personal elemental affinities can foster harmony, fulfillment, and deeper connections.

Recognizing our elemental nature is not merely a categorisation; it is a journey of self-discovery that enhances our understanding of what defines us. Whether we resonate with the kitchen's fiery passion, the bedroom's grounding stability, the living room's airy expansiveness, or the tranquil depths of the bathroom, embracing our elemental traits can transform our lives. This self-awareness strengthens our connections with ourselves and others and helps us navigate life with greater purpose, clarity, and authenticity.

CHAPTE 10
Diverse Ministerial Paths Aligned with Elemental Traits.

Understanding the ministerial callings that correspond to your elemental nature offers profound insight into the divinely endowed strengths that shape your service to the body of Christ. Just as creation is composed of four foundational elements—fire, earth, air, and water—each bearing distinct characteristics and purposes, your elemental alignment informs the unique way you are equipped to fulfill your calling and contribute meaningfully to the advancement of God's Kingdom.

Ministers aligned with the element of Fire are characterized by a dynamic and fervent approach to spiritual leadership. Drawing parallels with the prophet Elijah, who demonstrated divine authority through acts such as calling down fire from heaven (1 Kings 18:38), these individuals have a unique capacity to awaken spiritual urgency. Their ministry often emphasizes revival, holiness, and the prophetic proclamation of God's Word, confronting apathy and igniting renewed zeal among believers (2 Timothy 4:2).

Those whose ministry reflects the qualities of Earth embody stability, discernment, and doctrinal reliability. Like Jeremiah, whose prophetic mission was anchored in the realities of both divine truth and social responsibility (Jeremiah 1:10), earth-aligned leaders offer practical wisdom and structured teaching. Their emphasis on sound theology and spiritual maturity equips the Church with enduring foundations, promoting depth and resilience in faith communities (Ephesians 4:11–13).

Ministers resonating with the element of Air are often gifted in spiritual sensitivity and communication. Like the wind at Pentecost, which ushered in the Holy Spirit's transformative presence (Acts 2:1–4), these leaders operate with prophetic clarity and intuitive guidance. They cultivate spaces where believers encounter God through revelation and empowerment, fostering environments conducive to spiritual renewal and experiential faith (1 Corinthians 12:7).

Water-aligned ministers exemplify compassion, pastoral care, and relational leadership. Echoing Christ's servant-hearted gesture of washing His disciples' feet (John 13:5), they guide others with empathy and humility. Their influence is especially evident in counseling, mentoring, and fostering unity within the body of Christ. These leaders nurture spiritual growth through presence and patience, strengthening communal bonds and encouraging transformation (1 Peter 5:2–3).

Understanding one's elemental alignment in ministry not only enhances personal authenticity but also contributes to a more holistic expression of the Church's calling. Together, these diverse expressions of leadership—passionate (Fire), grounded (Earth), perceptive (Air), and nurturing (Water)—reflect the multifaceted nature of God's grace and purpose in the world.

The Prophetic Ministry and Elemental Traits: Understanding and Appreciating Their Significance

The prophetic ministry has always been an indispensable aspect of the Christian faith, characterized by spiritual insights and divinely inspired directions. However, many Christians have recently misunderstood and criticized this ministry. This uncertainty has arisen partly due to the visible excesses and abuses by some self-proclaimed prophets, which have overshadowed the genuine, God-ordained prophetic work. It is essential to recognize that prophets, as servants of God, operate under the guidance of divine wisdom and often use the elements—earth, fire, air, and water—to undertake spiritual directions and perform miracles. Understanding and appreciating their unique dimension of work requires a closer examination of their biblical foundations and the miraculous outcomes of their ministries.

The Element of Fire in Prophetic Ministry

Prophets have historically used various elements to execute God's directives, with fire being one of the most dramatic and powerful. For instance, the prophet Elijah, known for his fiery prayer life and dramatic miracles, evoked fire from heaven to consume the sacrifice on Mount Carmel. This event, recorded in 1 Kings 18:38 (NIV), states, *"Then the fire of the Lord fell and burned up the sacrifice, the wood, the stones and the soil, and also licked up the water in the trench."* This miraculous act was not just a display of divine power but also a clear direction from God to re-establish His sovereignty over Israel, proving His supremacy over the false gods worshipped by the people. Elijah's use of fire was a definitive act that displayed God's judgment and purification. In this context, fire stood for the intense, consuming nature of God's holiness and His power to cleanse and purify His people. Prophets aligned with the element of fire often embody similar characteristics—zeal, boldness, and an unyielding commitment to proclaiming the truth. Their ministries are marked by a zeal to confront sin, call for repentance, and invoke God's transforming power. This fiery passion can ignite revival, stirring hearts to return to God and live according to His commandments.

The Element of Earth in Prophetic Ministry

Similarly, prophets have used the element of earth to demonstrate God's power in more grounded, tangible ways. In one of His miraculous healings, Jesus used earth to heal a man born blind. John 9:6-7 (NIV) recounts, *"After saying this, he spit on the ground, made some mud with the saliva, and put it on the man's eyes. 'Go,' he told him, 'Wash in the Pool of Siloam.' So, the man went and washed and came home seeing."* Here, Jesus used mud—an earthly element—to heal, highlighting a miracle that needed a physical action tied to a spiritual directive. The use of the earth in this miracle symbolizes God's creation and restoration power. Just as God formed man from the dust of the ground, Jesus used the same element to restore sight to the blind man. Prophets who align with the element of the earth often focus on foundational, practical aspects of faith. Their ministries might emphasize teachings that ground believers in solid biblical doctrine, providing stability and growth. These prophets are instrumental in building robust and resilient faith communities rooted in the truth of God's word.

The Element of Air in Prophetic Ministry

The air element was notably present during the early apostles' meeting on Solomon's porch. Acts 2:2 (NIV) describes, "Suddenly a sound like the blowing of a violent wind came from heaven and filled the whole house where they were sitting."

This rushing wind symbolized the arrival of the Holy Spirit, empowering the early apostles to speak in various tongues. As an element, the air stood for a decisive move of the Holy Spirit, ushering in spiritual renewal and empowerment. Prophets aligned with the element of air are often highly attuned to the movements of the Holy Spirit. They excel in prophetic insights and communication. They create environments where the Spirit's power can flow freely, bringing believers renewal, healing, and empowerment. Their sensensitivity to the Spirit's leading allows them to deliver prompt and precise messages from God.

The Element of Water in Prophetic Ministry

Water is another element prominently used in prophetic ministry. In 2 Kings 5:10 (NIV), the prophet Elisha instructed Naaman, ***"Go, wash seven times in the Jordan, and your flesh will be stored, and you will be cleansed."*** Following his obedience to this divine instruction, Naaman's healing from leprosy illustrates how water, as a prophetic element, facilitated a miraculous cure, displaying God's multifaceted wisdom. Water is a significant element that resonates deeply with certain prophets. Like its refreshing and nurturing qualities, prophets associated with this element excel in pastoral ministry. Their deep empathy, compassion, and spiritual nourishment comfort and heal those in need, fostering unity, trust, and a sense of community among believers.

Embracing the Wisdom of Prophetic Directions

Understanding the prophetic ministry goes beyond intellectual knowledge; it requires embracing the divine wisdom it imparts. As Proverbs 8:12 (NIV) declares***, "I, wisdom, dwell together with prudence; I possess knowledge and discretion."*** This wisdom is revealed through the work of prophets, and it serves not only as a guiding force but also as a vital means of direction, emphasizing the importance of valuing their distinct contributions. Ecclesiastes 10:10

(NIV) further reinforces this principle: "*If the axe is dull and its edge unsharpened, more strength is needed, but skill will bring success.*" This verse illustrates that wisdom, often manifest through prophetic guidance—is invaluable and indispensable for fulfilling God's purposes. Prophets are intricately connected to the elements they employ as servants of God in their ministries. Their actions are not mere rituals; they carry spiritual significance and divine authority. Romans 1:20 (NIV) affirms this: *"For since the world's creation, God's invisible qualities—his eternal power and divine nature—have been seen, being understood from what has been made, so that people are without excuse."* Through their engagement with the elements, they reveal God's invisible qualities, making His divine nature clear to God's creation.

The Necessity of Discernment in Prophetic Ministry

While acknowledging the instances of excesses and abuses within the prophetic ministry, it is crucial to remember that these do not negate the authenticity and necessity of genuine prophets who faithfully serve God. The key to distinguishing between true prophets and those who may lead others astray lies in discernment. This discernment is a skill and responsibility each believer must take seriously. Rejecting the prophetic ministry entirely due to its abuses would mean overlooking a critical aspect of God's plan and wisdom for His people. When exercised properly, the prophetic ministry supplies clarity, direction, and empowerment to the body of Christ.They are vital in revealing God's heart and mind, guiding believers in fulfilling their destiny. Their unique ability to use the elements in their prophetic acts underscores the rich diversity of God's wisdom and his creative means of communication with His people. In harmony with the elements, the prophetic ministry reflects the multifaceted wisdom of God. They often harness natural elements—fire, earth, air, and water—as channels through which divine direction flows, resulting in miracles that testify to God's sovereignty and power. To fully grasp and honor their work, it is essential to acknowledge their heavenly calling and the scriptural foundation underpinning their actions. By doing so, we can discern the authentic prophetic voice from the false, ensuring we follow the path that aligns with God's will.

CHAPTER 11
Living Above The Elements

Understanding your elemental nature and personality traits is essential for navigating life with clarity and purpose. Everyone is shaped by elemental influences—fire, earth, air, and water—that contribute to their character, inclinations, and spiritual sensitivities. Gaining insight into these elements helps you understand your strengths, weaknesses, and how you engage with the world around you. However, it is essential to recognize that God's desire for you goes beyond simply understanding these elements; He wants you to rise above them. Living under the influence of the elements means being subject to their sway—whether it's the fiery passions that drive impulsiveness (fire), the stability and routine that define earthly desires (earth), the intellectual pursuits and social interactions that dominate (air), or the emotional depths and intuitive insights that guide actions (water). When you live under these influences, you may be limited by their constraints and vulnerabilities. But when you rise above them, you are empowered, confident, and extremely secure in God's plan. In Galatians 4:9-10, the apostle Paul warns the Galatians against returning to elemental principles. He emphasizes that living under the law—just as living under the sway of the elements—leads to bondage rather than the freedom found in Christ. This freedom, found in Christ, liberates you from the constraints of the elements and opens a world of hope and possibility. Similarly, yielding to these elemental influences can cause your decisions, emotions, and spiritual experiences to be dictated by these forces rather than by the higher life and freedom available through Jesus Christ. This stark contrast between living under elemental influences and living in the freedom found in Christ is a central theme of this piece, reinforcing the transformative power of embracing the prophetic ministry and living above elemental influences. It underscores the potential for spiritual growth and freedom.

A prime example of one such element that significantly influences human life is the moon, which is directly connected to the concept of lunacy. The term "lunacy" comes from the Latin word **lunar,** referring to the moon, and historically, it has been used to describe erratic behavior, mood swings, and psychological disturbances, often associated with the lunar cycles. This phenomenon, though controversial and not universally accepted as a scientific condition, suggests that the moon has a profound effect on human behavior, with some individuals becoming more susceptible to these influences during certain phases of the lunar cycle. The potential for the moon's sway to disrupt mental and emotional stability is a vivid illustration of how elemental forces, if not understood or controlled, can have a disruptive impact on one's well-being. Similarly, other natural elements, like the sun, exert their own influence on the human body, sometimes with harmful consequences. For instance, prolonged exposure to the sun's ultraviolet radiation can lead to severe skin damage and increase the risk of skin cancer. Both the moon and the sun—powerful natural forces—remind us that, while these elements are essential and influential in the world, their unchecked impact can lead to negative outcomes. This serves as a poignant reminder that, in the same way we seek to manage physical forces for health, we must also carefully guard against the spiritual and emotional forces that seek to dominate us, embracing instead the freedom that comes through Christ.

God's intention is not for His people to be subject to the harmful effects of these elements. Psalm 121:6-7 declares, ***'The sun will not harm you by day, nor the moon by night. The Lord will keep you from all harm and watch over your life.'*** This means God does not want the sun to smite you by day—that is, strike you with diseases like skin cancer—nor the moon to smite you by night, afflicting you with lunacy or psychological distress. Instead, He expects His children to rise above these influences and walk in the supernatural life that Jesus promised—Zoe, the higher life (John 10:10). This life is marked by spiritual vitality, divine wisdom, and mastery over natural forces, ensuring that one is not governed by the elements but by the Spirit of God.

Throughout Scripture, prophets have often used natural elements to convey divine messages, yet an over-reliance on these elements can lead to spiritual bondage, particularly if they become objects of fear, worship, or excessive attention. The prophetic ministry should always direct people back to God's sovereignty, reminding them that true security is found in Him, not in the manipulation or appeasement of natural forces. To live above these elements requires a transformation of mindset—a shift from reacting to external influences to proactively aligning with God's Word and Spirit. This divine alignment is not merely a theoretical concept but a tangible reality that offers peace amid chaos, security in uncertainty, and comfort in distress. When you live in God's presence, you are shielded from the adverse effects of natural forces. The Lord's watchful care ensures that no element, whether the scorching sun or the shifting moon, has power over your life. Thus, to truly overcome these influences, one must strive to be a mature son of God, constantly led and driven by the Spirit into a life of dominion and divine immunity.

While understanding your elemental nature can offer valuable insight, living a life transcending these influences is far more critical. As a child of God, you are called to walk in the freedom and authority Christ has secured. Embrace the supernatural life of Zoe, where you are empowered to rise above earthly limitations and live in alignment with God's divine purpose. This life is marked by spiritual discernment, peace beyond understanding, and unwavering confidence in God's love and provision. God calls you to live a life that reflects His divine nature and authority. You will experience His supernatural power in every single area of your life by rising above these earthly influences. Break free from the natural world's limitations and embrace life's fullness by walking closely with Him. In doing so, you will experience joy, peace, and fulfillment that can only come from stepping beyond the natural world and into the limitless possibilities of His kingdom. This life is filled with hope, inspiration, and the promise of a future shaped by God's divine purpose.

Mastery of the elements: Jesus' supernatural dominion

Jesus Christ, the Son of God, proves His supremacy over the natural world, consistently revealing His divine nature through out His earthly ministry as recorded in the Gospels. These accounts vividly depict His ability to operate beyond the limitations of natural laws, affirming His supernatural identity and purpose. One of His most remarkable displays is His walking on water. In Matthew 14:25-26 (NIV), we read: "*Shortly before dawn, Jesus went to them, walking on the lake. When the disciples saw Him walking on the lake, they were terrified. 'It's a ghost,' they said, and cried out in fear.*" This miraculous event defies gravity, showing His mastery over the water. Rather than sinking, He effortlessly traverses the stormy sea, underscoring His sovereignty.

Moreover, Jesus' command over the wind and the air offers further inspiration. In Mark 4:39 (NIV), amidst a violent storm on the Sea of Galilee, He rebukes the wind and commands the waves: "***He got up, rebuked the wind, and said to the waves, 'Quiet! Be still!' Then the wind ceased, and it was completely calm***." His immediate control over nature's chaos reveals His ability to restore peace and order.

Additionally, Jesus' power over life is demonstrated when He raises Jairus' daughter from the dead. In Luke 8:54-55 (NIV), we read: "***But He took her by the hand and said, 'My child, get up!' Her spirit returned, and at once, she stood up***." This act affirms His dominion over death and His mission to redeem humanity.

Jesus reveals His unparalleled mastery over creation through His miracles. His defiance of natural laws underscores His exceptional role as the Son of God and His divine purpose as the mediator between humanity and the Creator. As John 1:1-3 (NIV) states: "***In the beginning was the Word, and the Word was with God, and the Word was God. He was with God in the beginning. Through Him all things were made; without Him, nothing was made that has been made***." This passage from the Gospel of John reinforces Jesus' integral role in creating the universe and His mission to reconcile humanity with God.

Understanding the distinction between the Christian faith and other spiritual practices is vital, yet it is important to recognize that certain practices—such as meditation, rituals, and the invocation of spiritual entities—are not inherently evil. In fact, these practices can be found in Christian disciplines, albeit with a different focus and purpose. The question arises, however: why have individuals outside the Christian faith, such as monks or magicians, been able to maximize these practices to their fullest potential, achieving extraordinary feats like levitation or telekinesis, while many believers struggle to replicate or surpass such manifestations, despite engaging in similar practices?

These spiritual practices, when rooted in devotion to God and aligned with His will, hold the potential to lead believers into deeper encounters with His presence. Yet, the disparity between the power demonstrated by non-Christian practitioners and the limited manifestations in the lives of Christians can provoke a deeper inquiry. If the feats performed by these individuals are truly opposed to God's kingdom, as some suggest, why aren't Christians—empowered by Christ's authority, able to perform even greater miracles?

Scripture offers an answer. Jesus, in Luke 10:19, encourages believers to walk in His authority, enabling them to perform signs and wonders that bear witness to God's greatness. His words in John 14:12 further affirm that those who believe in Him will do even greater works. This raises a profound reflection: if we as Christians engage in these spiritual practices genuinely and with the right intentions, why do we not experience the same or greater manifestations as those outside our faith? The question is not whether these practices are evil, but why we have not fully embraced their potential within the context of our Christian walk. If we are to experience the fullness of what God has for us, we must examine whether we are truly engaging in these practices with the same depth and commitment as those who seem to unlock their full potential.

Furthermore, 1 Thessalonians 4:17 (NIV) speaks of believers being caught up in the air to meet the Lord during His second appearance: '*After that, we who are still alive and are left will be caught up with them in the clouds to meet the Lord in the air. And so, we will be with the Lord forever*.' This passage fills believers with a sense of anticipation and hope for the future, questioning why levitation, or being lifted into the air, should be viewed as unnatural or demonic when it is a part of the believer's ultimate hope in Christ.

Understanding God's sovereignty over creation can instill believers with a sense of confidence and courage. This yearning to transcend physical limitations and exercise dominion over creation resonates with the biblical mandate given in Genesis 1:28 (NIV), where God commands humanity to 'fill the earth and subdue it.' This instruction implies a divine calling to exercise authority over the natural world, which may include supernatural experiences in alignment with God's will. While it is crucial to exercise caution and discernment in evaluating supernatural experiences, Christians are encouraged to embrace a faith that includes the miraculous and pushes beyond the limits of the natural world. Through a biblical understanding of God's sovereignty over creation, believers can confidently exercise the authority bestowed upon them through Christ and experience His power here on Earth.

CHAPTER 12
The Legacy Of Remarkable Men And Women Of God

Throughout history, God's esteemed servants have exemplified unwavering faith, serving as vessels of His divine power. Their ministries were characterized by extraordinary signs, wonders, and miracles that profoundly impacted the global Church and contributed to the furtherance of His kingdom. These men and women are celebrated for their close walk with God, impact, and dedication to advancing His kingdom.

Joseph Ayo Babalola

Joseph Ayo Babalola, a pioneering figure in Nigeria's Pentecostal movement, became renowned for the remarkable manifestations of divine power that characterized his ministry. He is especially remembered for his extraordinary ability to raise the dead, heal the sick, and restore life to the lifeless—miracles that are well-documented and widely testified. Babalola also wielded authority over natural forces, famously commanding rain to cease during open-air gatherings, in a manner reminiscent of biblical prophets like Elijah. More significantly, he pioneered the Christ Apostolic Church and set the pace for the apostolic movement in Nigeria, igniting a nationwide revival that transformed countless lives and laid the foundation for many churches.

Benson Idahosa

Often regarded as the father of Pentecostalism in Nigeria,

Benson Idahosa embodied a ministry marked by bold faith and dramatic miracles. Through his prayers, severed limbs were restored, countless lives were healed and delivered to the glory of God. His pioneering spirit extended beyond Nigeria, making significant strides in spreading the Gospel across Africa and the globe. Idahosa's legacy inspires believers to anticipate God's intervention and foster an atmosphere of faith, hope, and expectancy for the miraculous.

Kathryn Kuhlman

Kathryn Kuhlman, an influential American evangelist, was distinguished by her sensitivity to the Holy Spirit and the manifest presence of God in her healing services. Miraculous recoveries, spiritual breakthroughs, and an extraordinary demonstration of the gifts of the Spirit marked her large-scale crusades. With astounding accuracy, Kuhlman diagnosed illnesses and performed instant healings. She left a legacy of faith that transcended denominational boundaries. Her ministry exemplified the ultimate power of God and continues to affect believers worldwide.

Smith Wigglesworth and Maria Woodworth-Etter

Smith Wigglesworth and Maria Woodworth-Etter were instrumental figures in the Pentecostal movement, known for their audacious faith and powerful demonstrations of God's might. Wigglesworth's ministry, grounded in simple yet profound trust in God, saw incredible healings and manifestations of divine power that inspired countless believers to expect miracles.

Maria Woodworth-Etter

Maria Woodworth-Etter, a pioneer preacher, gained widespread recognition for her powerful ministry of healing and prophecy. Her revival meetings attracted large crowds, where individuals experienced supernatural deliverance and encountered the tangible presence of God.

St. Joseph of Cupertino

St. Joseph of Cupertino (1603–1663), an Italian Franciscan friar and mystic, was known for his levitation experiences during states of ecstatic prayer. Witnesses, including fellow friars and church officials, documented these occurrences, interpreting them as evidence of his spiritual communion with God. Joseph's levitations contributed to his widespread reputation for piety and miraculous gifts.

St. Teresa of Avila

St. Teresa of Avila (1515–1582), a Spanish Carmelite nun and mystic, described levitation experiences during deep contemplation and union with God. In her writings, she reflected on these occurrences as divine encounters, highlighting the transformative power of prayer. Teresa's spiritual insights inspire seekers to deeper intimacy with God.

St. Francis of Assisi

St. Francis of Assisi (1181/1182–1226), founder of the Franciscan Order, is celebrated for his stigmata and extraordinary spiritual experiences. While reports of levitation in his life are rare, some accounts describe states of ecstatic prayer in which he transcended physical limitations. His life remains a testament to simplicity, humility, and a profound love for God and humanity.

Contemporary Accounts and Their Relevance

In contemporary times, occasional reports of supernatural phenomena, such as levitation, continue to surface within charismatic and Pentecostal movements, where they are often seen as manifestations of spiritual gifts and the tangible presence of God. These experiences are regarded by some as powerful signs of divine intervention and a deeper connection with the Holy Spirit. However, such claims often spark debate, as the evidence and interpretations vary widely. While some believe these phenomena are a continuation of the miraculous experiences once commonplace among saints, others argue that such occurrences have been dismissed or lost in more recent generations, leading many to view them as relics of a bygone era, no longer relevant to modern faith or practice.

Yet, if these encounters were integral to the spiritual journeys of early saints, why should present-day believers not seek similar experiences? Are we not also called to be His saints? Rather than relegating these phenomena to history, believers are encouraged to pursue a deeper connection with God and renew the faith that enables such divine manifestations. By committing to prayer, immersing ourselves in Scripture, and opening ourselves to God's Spirit, we can pioneer a revival of miraculous encounters that glorify God and strengthen the Christian community.

The lives of extraordinary individuals remind us that God's power is still accessible to those who earnestly seek Him. With unwavering faith and divine empowerment, believers today have the potential to surpass the spiritual accomplishments of their predecessors, ushering in life-changing revival in churches, communities, and nations.

CHAPTER 13
The Call To Greater Works

The pioneers of faith exemplified a life of intimate communion with God, showcasing His authority and power through remarkable acts that left a lasting impact on history. Figures such as John Wesley, Joseph Ayo Babalola, Benson Idahosa, and Kathryn Kuhlman exhibited unwavering trust in God, utilizing divine gifts to perform extraordinary feats—raising the dead, healing the sick, commanding natural forces, halting storms, and delivering prophetic messages that transformed entire communities. These acts vividly reflect the truth of Jesus' promise in John 14:12 (NIV): *"Very truly I tell you, whoever believes in me will do the works I have been doing, and they will do even greater things than these because I am going to the Father."* This declaration emphasizes the limitless potential of believers to walk in Christ's authority and perform works that surpass even His own earthly miracles. The lives of these transformative figures serve as a call to today's believers to pursue God wholeheartedly and to rise above the challenges that often inhibit the full manifestation of His power. By cultivating a deep, consistent relationship with God, nurturing steadfast faith, and embracing the miraculous, Christians can proclaim the Gospel with conviction and integrate the supernatural into their witness. As God's ambassadors, all believers are entrusted with the responsibility to reveal His reign and rule on earth. The stories of these faith pioneers affirm that ordinary individuals, when dependent on God, can become vessels for His extraordinary works. Their legacy serves as an inspiration, urging us to experience God's power personally and bring about lasting change through our faith. Today's believers are called to seek God's guidance, immerse themselves in Scripture, and pray for a fresh outpouring of His Spirit. However, the goal is not simply to replicate the feats of past generations but to surpass them by striving for an even deeper communion with God. Such devotion holds the potential to spark revival, reshaping churches, communities, and nations. By aligning ourselves with God's purposes and faithfully exercising the authority He has bestowed upon us, we honor the legacy of our predecessors and lay the foundation for future generations to experience the fullness of His power and love.